FENCING

BROWN

PHYSICAL EDUCATION ACTIVITIES SERIES

Consulting Editor:

AILEENE LOCKHART
University of Southern California
Los Angeles, California

Evaluation Materials Editor:

JANE A. MOTT
Smith College
Northampton, Massachusetts

PHYSICAL EDUCATION

ACTIVITIES SERIES

FENCING

MURIEL BOWER

San Fernando Valley State College

TORAO MORI

Retired Coach, Los Angeles Athletic Club
President United States Kendo Federation

WM. C. BROWN COMPANY PUBLISHERS
DUBUQUE, IOWA

Manufactured by WM. C. BROWN CO. INC., Dubuque, Iowa
Printed in U. S. A.

Preface

The primary objective of this book is to provide a concise, comprehensive source of information for students in college fencing classes, although its usefulness may well extend to any student of fencing.

Fencing is much too complex a sport to be learned from merely reading a book. Information presented here is not intended to serve as a complete "do it yourself" course, but is designed to reinforce and supplement the material covered in fencing classes.

The authors believe that the main emphasis in learning to fence should be on learning sound fundamental skills which are basic to the development of proficiency in fencing. They have attempted to set down the most complete information on foil fencing which can be presented within this limited space.

This book presents a brief background on the history and development of fencing, as well as a general overview of the sport. Reasons for various described techniques, on both the beginning and more advanced levels, are discussed in order to help the student understand the relative importance of each move as it is applied in a fencing situation.

Material in this book is up to date in terms of techniques, tactics, and rules. Electrical foil fencing is discussed, insofar as the electrical apparatus adds a new element to foil fencing. A chapter on the current rules of fencing has been included so that the reader can better understand some of the reasons behind the various skills and tactics he practices, so that he can perhaps be prepared to compete in classroom tournaments, and so that he can be a well informed spectator at a fencing tournament.

For the same reasons, basic officiating techniques for both standard and electric foil have been included.

Self-evaluation questions are distributed throughout these pages. These afford the reader typical examples of the kinds of understanding and levels of skill that he or she should be acquiring as progress is made toward mastery of fencing. The reader should not only answer the printed questions but should pose additional ones as a self-check on learning. Since the order in which the content of the text is read and the teaching progression of the instructor are matters of individual decision, the evaluative materials are not necessarily positioned according to the presentation of given topics. In some instances the reader may find that he or she cannot respond fully and accurately to a question until all the material has been read more extensively or more actual experience has been gained. From time to time therefore the reader should return to such troublesome questions until he is sure of the answers or has developed the skills called for, as the case may be.

Contents

The authors gratefully dedicate this book
to the memory of their fencing master of many years:

HENRI J. UYTTENHOVE

What Is Fencing?

Fencing is the historic art of offense and defense with the sword, in which the object is for one fencer to hit another without being hit first. Fencing developed into a true sport in the seventeenth century when gunpowder and firearms replaced the sword as the basic weapon. Swordsmanship then developed into a sport in which the objective became the touch and not the kill. Today much of the excitement and romance of the sport of serious duelling remain as the fencer attempts to protect himself from his opponent's point, while at the same time trying to find an opening in his opponent's defense.

Modern fencing has become a safe sport due to the protective clothing and flexible, blunted blade which are always used while participating in any "bouts." The objective of fencing is not to inflict an injury but to demonstrate an ability to outmaneuver and hit the opponent.

Fencing is now much faster and requires more refinement of technique than was possible with the heavier, longer, and stiffer weapons used by the earlier fencer.

The rules and manner of fencing reflect its original purpose even though techniques and tactics have undergone many changes through the years. There are three weapons which are used in fencing today: the foil, épée, and sabre.

FOIL

The foil, which was designed as a practice weapon, is the weapon with which this book is basically concerned. It is the only weapon which is used by women and is usually the first weapon a man learns to use as it is considered basic to fencing. This, naturally, does not mean that the foil is only a beginner's weapon to be discarded once a person becomes

How has sword fighting been modified so that it is one of the safest sports?

Evaluation Questions

proficient in its use, as the foil is probably the most difficult of the three weapons to master and offers a lifelong challenge to men and women alike. Once a man learns to use the foil well, he can readily learn to use the sabre and épée and many men enjoy competing in all three weapons.

Although the foil is blunted, it is theoretically a pointed sword capable of inflicting a puncture wound only. A "touch" is scored if the point of the blade hits any part of the valid target area, which is limited to the torso, from the collar to the groin lines in front, and on back and sides from the collar to hips. If the point lands anywhere else it is "off target" and is invalid. In foil, only those touches which in serious duelling would be potentially fatal are counted. There is no penalty for an off-target hit. Any point hit, valid or not, stops action and no subsequent hits may count until fencers have stopped and once more resumed fencing. A bout is ended when a fencer has been touched five times in a men's bout or four times in a women's bout.

In foil fencing a definite sequence of action should be followed. In such a "phrase d'armes" a well-executed attack, initiated by one fencer, must be parried or evaded before the defender can safely counterattack. This is a logical sequence of action when you consider that if someone were coming toward you with a sharp sword, your first consideration would be to defend yourself, then to hit in return. It would be dangerous to attack into an attack with sharp swords, as both fencers could be wounded or killed, so the rules do not favor this type of play.

SABRE

Sabre is related to the old cavalry sabre which men on horseback used as a cutting and thrusting weapon. Today's sabre is a triangular,

Evaluation Questions

What are the basic differences among the three types of fencing weapons?

Figure 1—Weapons: Sabre; Épée; Foil with a pistol grip; Electric Foil with a French grip

Figure 2—Fencer wearing the regulation uniform, including a metallic vest. The foil is electric

flexible, light blade with a theoretical cutting edge along the length of one side of the blade and one third of the opposite, or back, side. It also has a blunted thrusting point, so the sabre can be used either as a cutting or thrusting weapon. "Touches" are scored on the upper part of the body above a horizontal line drawn through the highest points of intersection of the thighs and the trunk of the fencer when in the "on-guard" position.

Sabre rules concerning right of way are similar to those governing foil in that the well-executed attack must be parried before a counter-attack is made. The sabre target is larger than that of the foil, with the arms and head also being valid targets so there is a great variety of actions possible than with foil. Movements are often larger than those of foil due to the enlarged target area and the cutting attacks common in sabre, but precise control is just as vital here as in the other weapons.

ÉPÉE

Épée more closely resembles real duelling than any other weapon. The épée, or duelling sword, is stiffer and heavier than the foil, but is still a point or thrusting weapon. Points anywhere on the body are valid and there is no definite sequence of play which must be followed. The first person to hit scores, and if two fencers hit simultaneously both are declared touched.

ELECTRICAL WEAPONS

The difficulty in accurately judging hits by sight has led to the development of effective electric scoring devices in foil and épée. Electric sabre has not yet been perfected to the point of being practical, but will undoubtedly be in use in the not too distant future.

The épée machine has been in use for many years. The foil machine was first used for a major international tournament in the 1955 World Championship meet. Both electric foil and épée are now required in all major meets.

Electrical épées and foils have a "button" at the tip which is depressed when a touch is made, and records the touch by means of a light and buzzer on a central machine. In electrical épée, only a simple circuit is needed since a point may land anywhere on the body. In foil, however, the problem is complicated by the limited valid target area and by the possibility of off-target hits. Electrical foil scoring machines were slower to develop than épée because the machine has to differentiate between fair and foul touches, but this was finally accomplished. Over their regular jackets, foil fencers must wear a metallic jacket which covers only the valid target area. The machine registers with a colored light if the point lands on the valid area and a white light if the point lands anywhere "off-target."

FENCING SCHOOLS

In the seventeenth century the need for fencing instruction increased as the popularity of duelling grew among the aristocracy. The most important fencing schools originated in Italy, France, and Spain. Each used a different system and each was considered to be superior by its proponents. The Italian and French systems of fencing proved to be the most widely accepted through the years and today the influences of these two schools can still be seen. Modifications throughout the years have brought the Italian method which relied more on power, and the French method which relied more on finesse, closer together until now the major difference is in the shape of the handle, which affects the use of the foil.

In this book the French foil is the weapon considered. Although any handle can be used similarly, the French handle calls for more finesse and control and is the more balanced foil, making it less tiring to hold. The other grips tend to be more powerful but have a shorter, lighter handle, making the weapon point-heavy and so more fatiguing to hold. Some fencers strap these shorter grips to their wrists for added support, but this limits freedom of movement.

WHO FENCES TODAY?

In Europe fencing has traditionally been, and still is, a major sport. It is the Western Europeans who have been consistent winners in international tournaments, although in recent years Poland, Hungary, and Russia have dominated Olympic and World Championship events. In these countries children begin fencing at an early age and the best of these continue to fence throughout their lifetimes.

In America, fencing is a fast growing sport with more and more active participants each year. There are fencing clubs and salles in every major city in the United States where men, women, and children can learn to fence and continue to practice.

An ever-increasing number of colleges and high schools are offering fencing as more and more people realize the fascination of this sport. Fencing is an excellent carry-over sport and many people who first became interested in it during their school years continue for years afterwards. Since it is a sport which can be enjoyed by men, women, and children, it is not uncommon to find whole families enjoying this activity together.

VALUES OF FENCING

Fencing is a vigorous sport which requires and develops stamina, quick reactions, speed and accuracy of movement, and excellent coordination.

Fencing is also a mental game. Once a fencer has practiced the various movements until he is physically able to carry out a plan without having to think about how the various parts of the body must move, he finds that the real excitement lies in outthinking and outwitting his opponent. You must quickly analyze your adversary's style and then plan your strategy accordingly. You must set traps for your opponent while being careful to avoid those set by him.

In addition to a keen, analytical mind, fencing requires decisive thinking and the courage to assume the offensive at any instant that an opportunity arises. If a fencer delays in building up the courage to move, the exact moment will be lost. By being prepared to move at any time, by forcefully dominating your opponent, and by successfully carrying out your plans, self-confidence is increased.

Good sportsmanship is an integral part of fencing tradition. Fencing was for many years considered a sport for gentlemen only, and participants were expected to conduct themselves accordingly. Much of this "flavor" still exists. For instance, etiquette requires that a fencer must acknowledge all touches against himself in practice, and that any doubtful touches must be refused by the one who attempted to score.

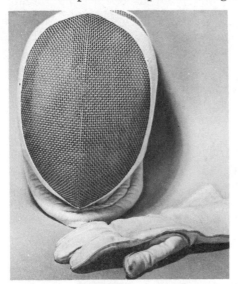

Figure 3—Mask and glove

EQUIPMENT YOU WILL NEED

Fencing equipment is relatively inexpensive and long lasting. You will need at least one foil. For protection you must always wear a strong mask and a padded white jacket, or a half-jacket when you practice.

It is also advisable to wear a fencing glove on the sword hand for protection and as an aid in gripping the foil. A regulation foil glove is made of leather, is padded on the back, and is long enough to cover the end of the jacket sleeve so that the opponent's point cannot go inside the sleeve. Any glove may suffice for the beginner, but it is wise to accustom yourself to fencing with a glove from the start.

Men and women both wear white trousers which must be long enough to cover the knee and loose enough to allow freedom of movement. Add white socks and tennis shoes and you are ready to fence.

SAFETY

It is always a mistake to cross blades with anyone unless you are both wearing a mask and a jacket which protects the body, the foil arm, and the neck. Accidents can happen to the unprotected fencer very easily as a fencer can be responsible for only his own careful actions. Once a second person is involved you cannot know exactly how he will move or react, and a well trained fencer is apt to react reflexively to a fast moving blade in such a way as to endanger his or his opponent's face.

COLLEGE FENCING

The college fencing season may extend from October or November through the third weekend in March, at which time the men's N.C.A.A. Fencing Championships are held as a climax to the fencing season. For many years the Eastern colleges and universities have dominated collegiate fencing, but intercollegiate fencing programs for men and women are increasing in number and strength throughout the entire country.

AMATEUR FENCERS LEAGUE OF AMERICA

This organization governs all fencing tournaments in this country. Divisions have been established throughout the nation to administer local fencing groups and tournaments.

Regularly scheduled tournaments for women, and in all three weapons for men, are held within these divisions from September to June. Divisional winners in all open events qualify for the national championships which are held annually in the latter part of June. National rankings and Olympic Team membership are determined from the results of divisional and national championship tournaments.

INTERNATIONAL FENCING

All international fencing falls under the jurisdiction of the Federation Internationale d'Escrime, with which the A.F.L.A. is closely affiliated. United States fencers have gained much international prestige over the years. Although this country has not won any Olympic fencing events, it has had finalists and medalists in every weapon. Miguel A. de Capriles served as president of the F.I.E. from 1960-1964, the first American to be so honored.

Skills Basic to Fencing

Since fencing positions are unlike those of any other sport, it is essential that the beginner take the time necessary to practice the basic moves until they become automatic, thus freeing the mind to think in terms of acting and reacting to a second, often unpredictable, person.

Although some individual differences are bound to occur, sound basic fencing skills relate to ultimate success in fencing. Various positions and movements have been developed and modified over hundreds of years, so that each position and each action serves a definite purpose. While fencing movements are not difficult, they can become automatic only by continuous repetition. Practicing in front of a capable critic or a mirror is a good way to begin.

At first you will find the foil feels awkward and unwieldly, but as you become used to its feel it will become a part of you as you fence. Your movements will tend to be too large at first also, but with practice these will become small and fast.

THE FOIL

The foil consists of a rectangular blade and its mounting. The blade is 35″ in length, with the over-all foil being about 42″ long. The blade tapers from the strong half near the handle, which is called the "forte," to the weaker, more flexible half, which is called the "foible." The "forte" is used for the defense since it is thicker and more rigid than the tip end of the blade. The tip itself is blunted and must be covered with a rubber tip or with white tape. Foil blades come in sizes from one to five, size one being the shortest. Most adults use a number five blade, but some

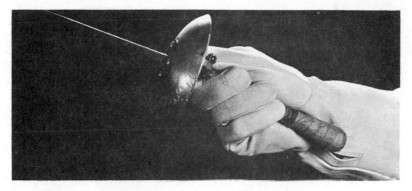

Figure 4—How to hold the foil

prefer to sacrifice an inch in length for the improved balance and maneuverability of the shorter number four blade.

The mounting consists of the guard, or bell, a thumb pad, the handle, and the pommel, which acts as a counterbalance.

HOW TO HOLD THE FOIL

The rectangular French handle is not straight. The right-handed foil should be held so that, with the wider sides on the top and bottom, the handle will curve upward and to the right near the guard.

With the handle in this position, place the last joint of the thumb on top, about ½ inch from the guard. Place the second joint of the forefinger on the bottom so that it opposes the thumb. It is with these two fingers that you will guide the foil.

The remaining three fingers should wrap around the handle with the tip of the little finger resting on the handle. The foil must be gripped lightly yet firmly, as a "heavy" or tense grip will result in large motions and will cause undue fatigue. The ability to manipulate the point with the smallest, quickest possible motions will depend on this relaxed but firm grip as the fingers guide the point. When you beat your opponent's blade, or when you defend yourself, you will find that your fingers must tense to provide additional force, but they must relax when your blade is once more free.

The pommel lies against the center of the wrist so that the foil becomes an extension of the arm with no up or down break at the wrist. *Note*: All directions will be for the right-handed fencer. Left-handed fencers should reverse these instructions.

Figure 5—First position of the
salute

Figure 6—First position of the
salute, side view

Figure 7—Second position of
the salute

Figure 8—Second position of the
salute, side view

THE ON GUARD POSITION

The Salute—Whenever fencers are about to cross blades, whether for a lesson, practice, or in a tournament, etiquette demands that they salute first, so the salute may be considered a standard preliminary to the on guard position, which is the basic stance preparatory to the attack, or for defense. To begin the salute, fencers face each other, foil in hand, and with the mask held under the left arm by the back piece, or tongue. The feet should be at right angles, with the right heel directly in front of the left heel and the right foot pointing in the direction of the other fencer. The left foot points to the side.

The salute is made in three quick, smooth motions. On count one, the foil arm is extended toward the floor; on count two the foil comes up so that the guard almost touches the chin, point up; and on count three, the sword arm is extended shoulder high, with the point aiming at your opponent. After this quick salute, the mask is put on with the left hand which is already holding it. The proper way to put the mask on is to put the chin in first so it rests on the chin pad, then pull the mask up and back over the top of your head in one quick motion. This method of putting on the mask not only looks nice but wastes very little time, and tends to pull your hair back away from your face, which is important to those who have hair long enough to hang in their eyes.

Figure 9—The On Guard Position

The Leg Position—You are now ready to assume the guard position in one motion. This stance will be broken down into its various parts so it can be learned bit by bit, but once you have become familiar with this position it should be quickly assumed after the salute.

The feet always remain at right angles with the right heel directly in front of the back one, but in the guard position the forward foot is moved ahead so that there is a space of about two of your foot lengths between the feet. Both knees bend so that they are over the toes with the body in the center, weight evenly distributed over the balls of the feet. In assuming this bent knee position be careful that only the legs move as you lower your body. The body must not lean forward or backward; the pelvis should be directly under the trunk and the shoulders level.

Can you identify the French and
the Italian foil?

Can you name the parts: A, B,
C, D?

Evaluation Questions
THE FOIL

The Arm Position—To bring the arm into position, the left arm is carried behind the head. It is bent at right angles, elbow shoulder high, hand relaxed and hanging forward about head height. In this position the left arm provides balance, helps keep the body in proper alignment, and is out of the way so it will not be hit. It will also, if kept in proper position, add impetus to the attack and act somewhat like a rudder, as you will see later on in the discussion of the lunge.

The right or sword arm is bent so that the elbow is about 8 inches in front of the body, with the hand held chest high and the point at the height of your opponent's eyes. You are now in the guard position.

In the guard position your body should be quite stable with no tendency to fall forward or backward, as you have lowered your center of gravity by bending your knees, and the wide stance gives you a firm base of support with your body balanced in the center, hips under the trunk.

The sideways stance puts the sword in front where you will be in position to get maximum reach in the attack and where the arm will help to protect you, as the right elbow should be front of your body. This position also narrows the target, but it is a mistake to take an extreme sideways position in order to further minimize the target. If you find you have difficulty in keeping the front foot and knee straight, you may turn the torso, from the pelvis up, to face slightly forward so that the knee and foot are in a natural position. An extreme sideways stance will restrict your attacking distance and will tend to cause your forward foot and knee to turn in. While such a stance offers a minimum target, it will also partially expose your back which is a valid target and is not as easily defended as the

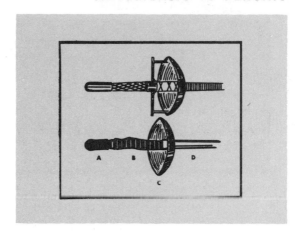

Diagram A:

THE FOIL

front of the target, making this not only an uncomfortable but an impractical position. If you come on guard, facing yourself in a mirror, your left hand should be just visible behind and beside your head.

FOOTWORK

The sport of fencing is only remotely related to the swashbuckling style of swordplay seen in the motion pictures, in which actors turn in circles, leap over tables, and swing from chandeliers. The surface on which you fence is called a "strip." It is 6 feet wide and 40 feet long, and fencers are free to move back and forth as long as they remain on the strip and do not reverse positions. Fencers are quite mobile on the strip and excellent endurance is required to fence for any length of time due to the speed of the footwork as the fencers move up and down the strip, each trying to draw the other a little too close, each keeping on the move so that the other cannot have a chance to get set to attack at leisure, and each trying to get the other a little off balance so a swift attack can be successfully launched.

Advance—The advance brings you closer to your opponent. It is made by moving the forward foot ahead first about one shoe length, with a heel-toe, walking step, then advancing the back foot the same distance. It is best to take short steps as you advance so you do not accidentally step into an attack or get too close to your opponent.

The advance is made in order to get close enough to attack if the opponent is out of distance. It may also be used to maintain a constant distance if the opponent has retreated or to force the opponent to retreat.

Figure 10—The Advance

The advance should be a fast, smooth, gliding motion. There should be no up or down bobbing of the head, no jerky leaping motions, and no dragging of the feet which will slow the footwork. The weight is carried on the balls of the feet and the back foot provides speed by pushing you forward as you advance.

1, Retreat—The retreat is the reverse of the advance. It is done by moving first the left foot back about one shoe length then the right foot. The feet should be the same distance apart at the end of the advance or retreat as they were originally.

The retreat may be used to make the opponent advance or to take you out of attacking distance as you defend against an attack. The retreat should also be made with a gliding motion.

2. Lunge—The lunge is the extension of the guard position; its purpose is to reach the opponent. It is the basic attacking position which brings you close enough to hit and in position for a quick recovery to the guard position at your regular fencing distance.

How to Lunge. All movements of the arm or blade must start with the point which is guided into the desired position by the thumb and forefinger. The lunge must also start with the point, which is aimed at the exact spot you hope to hit by pushing down on the handle with the thumb. Once the point is in line, the arm should be quickly and smoothly extended from the shoulder, with the hand slightly higher than the point. The shoulder must not be tensed or lifted as this will shorten your reach by at least an inch and cause your point to jump, spoiling your aim.

This smooth, fast extension should be practiced before practicing the lunge itself until it becomes natural and easy.

Figure 11.—The Lunge

Once the arm is working well, go on to the footwork of the lunge. Aim, extend the arm, then reach forward with the right foot and at the same time push your body forward with the back foot, which remains flat on the floor during the lunge in order to achieve greater stability. The main force of the lunge is provided by the powerful extension of the left leg which drives you forward. The left leg works much like a strong spring which is compressed as you crouch in the guard position, and hurls you forward as the spring, your leg, is released. The driving force which propels you forward must push forward through the hips, never up and forward.

At the same time the left leg extends, the left arm is flung down and back so that it is in line with, and parallel to, the left leg, palm up. This backward extension of the arm helps provide force to the lunge and is a vital part of the lunge as it quickly displaces your body forward. If the left arm moves sideways when you lunge, you will find that you can easily lose your balance in the direction the arm moves. The arm extends straight down.

At the end of the lunge your body should be in the following position: right knee bent directly over the right instep, not over or in front of the toe as this will put undue strain on the knee and thigh and slow your recovery; hips still under the trunk, facing almost forward; trunk straight but leaning a little toward the point; shoulders level; both arms and left leg straight; left foot flat on the floor.

15

What three errors has the fencer in diagram B committed in the lunge?

How have the mistakes weakened his effectiveness?

Evaluation Questions

THE LUNGE

Figure 12—The Development of the Lunge

Recovery from the lunge is made by pushing backward forcefully from the right heel as the left leg and both arms return to the guard position. Be sure to bend the left leg on recovery so you will be in your beginning stance, never standing upright. It takes much less energy to return to a crouch position than to a standing one, and only in this lower position are you ready to continue fencing, which may be necessary if your attack did not land.

At first the lunge should be made slowly and analyzed at each step until you are sure you understand how to lunge correctly. You will need to stretch gradually until you can perform a full, deep lunge without feeling any strain. As soon as you can do this slowly, you should begin working for speed and force which can be acquired only through continuous repetition. Many top ranking fencers lunge at least 100 times daily to keep themselves flexible, fast and in good condition.

Diagram B:

THE LUNGE

Fencers today rarely remain static on the strip. You will need to be able to cover ground quickly, either forward or backward, so the advance, retreat and lunge should be practiced until they become natural movements for you. Then try various combinations of these actions.

Advance-Lunge—In an advance-attack the sword arm must be extended at the start of the advance, since this is the beginning of the attack, and it must remain extended throughout the attack. Any time the arm is withdrawn during an attack, the attacker may be hit by a quick thrust from the other fencer, so to make this attack you should first extend as you start to advance, then lunge with no hesitation between movements.

Figure 13—Advance-Lunge

It often is necessary to attack in this way since much fencing today is done out of distance, so a lunge will not reach the opponent. This is a safer distance for fencing since it gives more time for the defense, but it does require the ability to cover this distance with great speed.

The advance attack is also useful against the opponent who, though perhaps in fencing distance, habitually retreats as you attack, thereby necessitating the extra distance gained in the initial advance. It is essential that you keep all parts of your body under control throughout any actions you make. If you over-lunge or lose your balance in any way it may be relatively easy for your opponent to score; so while all-out speed and determination are required in the attack, your body must always be controlled by keeping the left foot firmly on the floor during the lunge and by balancing correctly.

Lunge, Recover Forward, Lunge—If your opponent has retreated just out of reach as you lunge, you may recover forward from the lunge by bending the left leg and bringing it forward to put you in the guard position, from which you can defend, advance to a better position, or immediately lunge again to score.

You may now try any combination of these actions: advance-lunge-recover forward-lunge; advance-lunge-recover backward-retreat; etc.

FENCING DISTANCE

Fencing distance, or the distance between two fencers, depends on the length of the lunge. Fencers should be far enough apart so that a full lunge can just reach the opponent. You should never be on guard closer than this distance or you will be too easily scored upon, but you may fence farther apart if you desire. It is important that you quickly become accustomed to your lunging distance so that you will not make the mistake of fencing too close, a mistake common to beginners. If one fencer has a longer lunge than the other, you should fence at the distance of the longer reach.

ENGAGEMENT

Contact of the foibles of the blades for protection while in the guard position is called "engagement" of the blades. When fencers are lunging distance apart, it is safest to engage blades, usually in four or six. If the other blade is to the left of yours, you would move to four so that a simple lunge could not land against you, and if the blade is to the right of yours, you would move to six to protect that line. If two right-handers or two left-handers are working together they will both be engaged in the same line.

In the engagement, contact should be made lightly with no pushing of the blades. With this light contact, your fingers are sensitive enough to feel the slightest movement made by your opponent's hand before you can see the motion.

Lines of Engagement—The target is theoretically divided into four "lines," or sections: high-inside, high-outside, low-inside, and low-outside. The upper lines are above the foil hand and the lower lines below the hand. The inside lines are toward the front of the body, or to the left of the sword hand for right-handers, and the outside lines are toward the back, or to the right of the sword hand. The hand moves left or right as necessary to protect the target.

There are two guard positions for each line: one with the hand in supination, in which the palm faces up, and one in pronation, or palm down. The supination parries are the ones usually used in foil fencing,

Figure 14—Hand in the Fourth Position

Figure 15 — Front View of the Guard of Fourth, Protecting the Upper-Inside Line

19

while the pronation parries are used most often in sabre. With the four supination positions you can readily protect any area of the target.

Four. The high-inside line is that of "four," or "quarte." The hand moves to the left until it is in front of the left side of the body, point over the edge of the opponent's right shoulder. In this position, the wrist breaks laterally so the pommel is not against the wrist, but the handle remains under the base of the thumb. The thumb is on top of the handle.

Six. The high-outside line is "six," or "sixte." The hand moves to the right so that it is in front of the right side of the body, point over the opponent's left shoulder. This tends to be a weaker position than four for many people, much as the backhand stroke in tennis is often weaker than the forehand. In order to assure a strong six position, rotate the hand slight-

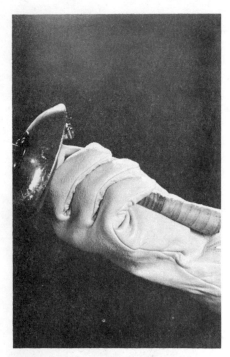

Figure 16—Hand in the Sixth Position

Figure 17 — Front View of the Guard of Sixth Protecting the Upper-Outside Line

ly to the right so that the knuckle of the thumb is directly to the side, and brace the pommel against the inside of the wrist for additional support. In this position there should be a straight line from the elbow through the foil.

SEVEN. "Seven," or "septime," defends the low-inside line. From the high lines of four or six, the move to seven is made by breaking the wrist downward as the point moves clockwise, stopping just beyond the opponent's knee. The hand is to the left of the body as it was in four, still chest high with the palm of the hand facing up.

EIGHT. The guard of "eight," or "octave," defends the low-outside line. From four or six, the blade moves counterclockwise, stopping at the inside of the opponent's knee. The hand pivots to the new position as the

Figure 18—Hand in the Seventh Position

Figure 19 — Front View of the Guard of Seventh, Protecting the Lower-Inside Line

How could this engagement be changed from six to four?

Should the point or the hand move first to the new position?

Evaluation Questions

CHANGE OF
ENGAGEMENT

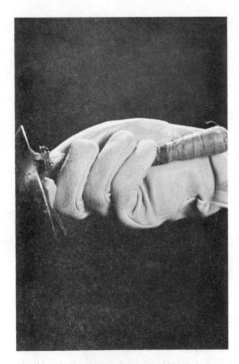

Figure 20—Hand in the Eighth Position

Figure 21 — Front View of the Guard of Eighth Position, Protecting the Lower-Outside Line

Diagram C:

CHANGE OF
ENGAGEMENT

wrist breaks down, palm of the hand up. The hand does not move down.

FINGERING. Fingering refers to the manipulation of the foil tip by the action of the thumb and forefinger only. It is essential for a good fencer to be able to move the point in this manner so that there will be no superfluous motion which is time consuming and enables the opponent to more easily see what you are doing.

Change of Engagement is made by passing the point of the foil under the opponent's blade to engage it on the opposite side. The point must move the smallest possible distance with very delicate fingering. The point should move first to contact the other side of the blade, then the hand moves to the new guard position.

The change is useful in maintaining control over your opponent's foil. If, for instance, you feel that the other fencer is about to attack, a quick change of engagement may upset his plans.

Double Change of Engagement consists of two rapid changes of line without moving the hand. A proficient fencer often attacks as his opponent advances, since for a brief instant he cannot retreat out of distance. A quick double change as you advance makes it very difficult for the other person to attack. The double change can be used in the same way that a single change is made. These actions should both be used, but not continuously. Remember that you must always keep the opponent guessing as to what you will do next, so be careful to avoid doing any one thing repeatedly.

The double change is good fingering practice as it strengthens the fingers. It also requires a relaxed grip and so can serve as a reminder to keep the hand and arm loose as you fence.

DEFENSE

Parries—The defense with the blade is called a "parry." This may be either a "blocking" parry, which is made by moving the sword to protect yourself by blocking the attack, or by a beat, which is made by spanking the blade sharply. The blocking-parry is more useful against a powerful attack, against a fencer who is too close, or against one who tries to hit by jabbing repeatedly. The beat-parry is more useful against a clean attack as it frees your blade so that you may immediately score after your defense.

Either type of parry is made by moving the point and hand to the desired line, so that you may parry in four, six, seven, or eight. There must be no backswing and no follow-through, either of which would momentarily expose your target and consume additional time. The flexible tip of

Figure 22—A Defender Moves from the Guard of Six to Parry in Four

the blade whips laterally at any sharp impact, but it will quickly right itself if the hand is kept under careful control. Any large motions will result in still more point deviation, making it very difficult to guide the point accurately. You must try to stop the point just over the edge of your opponent's shoulders in the high lines, or beside the knee in the low lines. From the proper parry positions, one need only aim the point and quickly extend to score after a successful defense.

When making a parry, the sword arm should neither extend nor bend from the guard position unless the opponent is closer than the normal fencing distance, in which case the arm will have to be withdrawn in order to parry. All parries should deflect the opponent's blade to the side, never up or down for this may result in a foul hit to the legs or head. The target is longer than it is wide, so the quickest, shortest parry is lateral.

Types of Parries—

DIRECT PARRIES are made by moving the sword to the left or right to defend either the high or low lines. If a fencer is on guard in six, the line of four will be open, so an attack to the line of four may be defended by the direct parry of four.

SEMICIRCULAR PARRIES are made when moving from high to low or from low to high lines, since the tip of the blade describes an arc as it crosses the body to remove the threatening blade laterally.

CIRCULAR, OR "COUNTER" PARRIES are made by changing lines with a small, circular motion of the blade, so that an attack to the high-inside line of four can be parried by the direct parry of four, or by counter-six.

While the circular parries may seem to be slow, they can be made very quickly. For instance, if a fencer is on guard in four, the high-outside line of six will be unprotected, so an attack to this open line can be parried with counter-four. Since the hand is already in the position of four, the arm need not move. The thumb, forefinger, and wrist will guide the point under the blade to pick it up in four with a quick, small, powerful parry.

It is important for a fencer to be able to make either a direct or counter-parry in any line and to vary his use of them. You will find that any time a fencer can accurately predict what you will do, that is, how you will attack or parry, he can score, so outwitting your opponent is a major part of fencing. Changing your defense is one way of keeping the other person guessing, thereby making it more difficult for him to plan his attack.

ATTACKS

Hitting the Opponent—Before actually attacking another person, it is important to learn to make a "soft hit" as opposed to a "hard" or jabbing hit.

The action which hits the opponent is called a *thrust*. It is advisable to first thrust at a wall target by taking the guard position just far enough away so that, by extending your arm, you will reach the target firmly enough to cause the blade to bend slightly upward. Once the feeling of thrusting with the arm is acquired, the same thing can be tried from

*Figure 23—The Thrust. The Arm Is
Extended with the Hand Shoulder
High and the Point Slightly Lower
Than the Hand*

the full lunging distance. The thrust should be firm and quick but not hard.

When you are thrusting well with a full lunge, do the same thing against another person. As soon as possible you must develop the feel of placing the point on the target with the fingers, and you must learn to be hit without flinching. A good way to practice at first is for partners to get on guard, lunging distance apart, and to take turns lunging and hitting each other with no attempt being made to defend. Later the defense may be added as attacks gain in speed and skill.

Simple Attacks are those consisting of only one fast action. These attacks rely on speed and surprise or timing. There are three simple attacks.

STRAIGHT THRUST. This is a fast lunge with no change of line during the attack. It is occasionally a very good attack but cannot be used often against a good fencer.

The straight thrust can be used against an opponent who is not protected in the guard position. Fencers often fence with "absence of the blade," which means that they do not engage blades while on guard but leave the line to which the opponent's blade points unprotected. This is most common when fencing out of distance or more than lunging distance apart. If you can maneuver such a fencer to within fencing distance it is often possible to score with an explosive straight thrust.

DISENGAGE. When the line in which you are engaged is "closed," or protected, you may change lines to hit with a disengage. This is made by guiding the point under the opponent's blade with the fingers making the smallest motion needed to clear the blade, then reaching and lunging. This should be made as one continuous motion. The blade stays close to the opponent's blade so that the action will be fast and difficult to see. You may disengage from any line to any other line, low or high, but when changing from seven to eight, or from eight to seven, the disengage will be made over the blade rather than under.

Hitting with Opposition. If fencers are engaged in four, their hands are to the left of their torsos. When one makes a disengage to six, the hand should change to the position of six when the arm extends so that the attacker's blade opposes the defender's blade, thereby protecting the attacker's target during the attack.

Care must be taken to make the line change before lunging so that there will be no tendency to withdraw the arm during the attack.

Cut-Over, or Coupé. The cut-over consists of lifting the point until it just passes over the other blade, extending, and lunging, all in a continuous motion, with the blade in opposition. This may be effective against a slightly low but not a threatening point, or when the opponent applies pressure to your blade.

Compound Attacks—Any attack which is made up of two or more actions is a compound attack. In such an attack, there will be one or more preparatory actions followed by the final or thrusting part of the attack. In any such attack, the attacker gains right of way by extending his arm and loses it if he bends his arm during the attack, so in these attacks the arm must remain extended.

Preparatory Actions

Feint. This is a motion which is intended to look like an attack. It is made to cause a reaction which will open the line to which the real attack will be made and it is made by extending the foil arm without moving the rest of the body. A feint may be made to any line, so you may feint a straight thrust, feint a disengage, or feint a cut-over. The feint must be fast and decisively made or it will not fool the opponent into thinking it is the real attack.

Beat. This is similar to a beat-parry, except that as an offensive action the beat is made with the foible against the foible. It is made with a clean, sharp, spanking action to either side of the blade. The beat may be very strong to open the line to be hit, or it may be a light beat to cause an answering beat from the opponent, thereby opening the opposite line for a disengage attack. The beat must be made close to the blade with no backswing or follow-through which would expose your own target.

Press. The press is similar to the beat, but is a more subtle action. The fingers grip the handle forcefully to push, or press, the other blade. There should be no arm or hand motion and the point must not move out of line, but must be kept under control for the action which is to follow. Usually this is done to cause the opponent to press in return, and may be followed by a disengage or cut-over.

Figure 24—The One-two Attack. Fencers Are on Guard in Six

Figure 25—The One-two, Continued. The Fencer on the Right Begins the Attack as He Drops His Point Under the Other Blade to . . .

Figure 26—The One-two Continued. . . . feint to the open line of four

Figure 27—The One-two Attack ends with a Final Disengage to the Line of six as the Defender Moves to Parry the Feint to the Fourth Line

Glide. This consists of gliding the blade along that of the opponent as the arm extends. It is similar to the feint and is useful against a light hand.

Derobement, or Deceiving a Parry. As the opponent attempts to parry your blade in answer to a beat, you may drop your point just low enough for the parry to pass over your blade without hitting it, then attack.

Two Examples of Compound Attacks—By combining one or more preparatory actions before the final thrust, you can make a wide variety of such attacks.

ONE-TWO. This consists of: feint a disengage, deceive the direct parry and disengage to score.

DOUBLE. This consists of: feint a disengage, deceive the counter-parry, and lunge. If the opponent parries a feint with a counter-parry, it may be deceived by continuing around the blade to hit in the line to which the feint was made. This is a corkscrew type of attack which describes a circle and a half.

SOME OTHER EXAMPLES OF COMPOUND ATTACKS FOLLOW: beat or press, and straight-thrust, disengage, or cut-over; beat in the opposite line, and straight thrust, cut-over, or disengage; feint any simple attack and disengage.

Attacks usually should not consist of more than two or three movements because an attack which takes too long to execute may be stopped before its completion by a counteraction from your opponent. Often the simplest attacks, made with great speed and accuracy at just the right time, are the most effective ones.

Attacks in Advance—When you fence out of distance, or when you feel certain that your opponent will retreat out of distance as you advance, you may advantageously make an advance attack to bring you within scoring distance. A short fencer must master this particular kind of attack in order to compensate for a shorter lunging distance. Any compound attack of two or three actions can be effectively made in advance. The feint, beat, or press is made as you advance, with the final thrust being made as you lunge.

As an example, the one-two attack in advance is made by feinting a disengage while advancing, then making the final disengage while lunging. In any advance attack which involves a feint, care must be taken to maintain an extended arm position throughout the entire attack. Withdrawal of the arm during any part of the attack loses the right-of-way for the attacker so that the defender's quick extension, at the instant the arm bends, will take the right-of-way from the attacker.

Techniques for the Better Fencer

When the ability to perform the basic techniques is acquired, there are more advanced techniques that may be progressed to which will provide a greater variety for your game.

ADVANCED FOOTWORK

The Ballestra is similar to the advance-lunge, but a light, quick jump replaces the two-count advance, making the ballestra quicker than the advance-lunge. The foil arm extends as the jump begins. The jump is made by pushing with the left foot as the right foot reaches forward. The attacker lands in the guard position with the left foot about where the right foot was at the start of this action. The body weight is taken only momentarily on the forward toe, which, along with the extension of the left leg, pushes to provide impetus for the lunge which follows immediately. The push for the ballestra should be forward so that the attack will just skim over the surface of the strip.

This is best done with a two-part, compound attack such as the one-two, beat-disengage, etc., as it is easy to coordinate the two counts of jump-lunge with such an attack. This is a valuable skill for the shorter person to master, but it is useful for any fencer who must attack from out of distance.

The Flèche, or running attack, is an advanced skill which can be used effectively but should be used sparingly. This is a swift attack which must be made very suddenly with no telegraphing motions so that it will surprise the opponent. It can be described as a "do-or-die" attack as it is an all-out attack in which the attacker runs past the other fencer as he attempts to score. To do this the attacker extends his arm as he drives his body forward with the right toe, then leads forward with the left foot which passes beyond the right foot, and continues running past his opponent. Care must be taken to run past, never into the other fencer for this could be dangerous to both fencers and is clearly forbidden in the rules of fencing. The attacker must allow his sword arm to relax with the hit to lessen the danger of breaking the blade. If this attack fails, the attacker may not continue fencing because action must stop as soon as one fencer passes another.

This attack is best made with a two-part attack. The defense consists of a firm blocking parry made in retreat.

The flèche should never be made against an opponent who is inclined to stop-thrust or advance into an attack. It is best made against an opponent who likes to retreat. It should not be used often since its main advantage lies in surprise, and since the attacker is unable to stop or change direction once he has begun the attack.

ATTACKS TO THE BLADE

Any action which deflects the opponent's blade from the target, thereby clearing the way for an attack, is an attack to the blade. The beat and press were discussed in Chapter 2, but there are two additional attacks to the blade which should be mentioned. The bind and the croise are very useful actions which remove a menacing point and, if properly done, continue to score.

The Bind is made only against an extended arm with a menacing point. The extended arm should be fairly rigid so that the opponent's entire arm and sword act as a lever. This action carries the blade from high line to low line where the attacker scores with a hit made in opposition to the blade, thereby assuring the attacker protection during this action. To make a bind, the attacker meets the foible of the opponent's blade with the forte of his own in four or six. If it is met in four, the point is guided over the opponent's blade and downward to score as the extending arm and hand moves to eight. From an engagement of sixth, the blade would pass over and downward to the position of seven. This must be very quickly done in one strong motion so that the other blade will be controlled throughout the attack.

This action, if very powerfully executed, can be used successfully to disarm an opponent, but there is no longer any advantage in doing so as action stops when a foil is dropped.

What attack to the blade is B using?

Is he correct in choosing this technique when A's arm is straight?

How can A defend himself?

Evaluation Questions

ATTACKING TO
THE BLADE

The defense against the bind consists of bending the foil arm to parry in seven or eight, depending on which side the attack is arriving. If the attacker is not quick enough or telegraphs his intent, it is not difficult to evade the attempt to bind by passing the point underneath the would-be-attacker's blade, arm still extended and point in line.

The Croise is made in much the same way as the bind, but is made against a straight arm attack which brings the opponent's blade so close to the target that a complete bind is dangerous for it brings the blade across the body. If the opponent is close the croise is better as it moves the opponent's extended arm from four to seven so that the blade does not cross your own target.

VARIATIONS OF THE ATTACK

Change of Tempo—The list of attacks which was discussed in Chapter 2 need not be expanded, but these attacks may be made more effective by varying the timing used in their execution.

The one-two or double, for instance, can be made by making a definite, but slightly slower, longer feint than usual, followed by a sudden burst of speed as the final disengage is made, thereby upsetting the timing of the defense. This principle can be effectively applied to any attack. The disengage may be explosively fast or a very subtle, sliding attack which is deceptively slow.

The False Attack is similar to a feint and is used for the same reasons, but it is made with a partial or full lunge. It must look like an attack, but fall just short. It is done to provoke a response from an opponent which

Diagram D:

ATTACKING TO
THE BLADE

will, in turn, lead to the conclusion of the attack. Such an attack is often referred to as an "attack on second intent."

The false attack can be used against a person who often makes a stop thrust into your attack. With the false attack, the stop comes out and the attacker then makes a quick parry of the stop and continues to hit. In this instance the arm must be withdrawn very little for the parry, and the parry must be very small so that the final attack will have only a few inches to travel before hitting, making this a very hard attack to parry.

When you fence against a person who makes many second intent attacks, the best defense is to retreat and make a decisive blocking parry.

COUNTERATTACKS

Counterattacks are offensive actions made on attacks.

The Stop Thrust is a straight thrust, with or without a lunge, depending on the distance the thrust must travel to hit, into the opponent's attack or advance. It should be made only when the adversary leaves the blade, makes feints in which the point moves out of line, or withdraws his arm in advance. It should be made at the instant the opponent's foot lifts to advance.

The stop is never a defense against a well-executed attack, but takes the time from an imperfect attack. The stop must be made as the opponent's blade moves out of line on a wide feint or as his arm bends during a composed attack or in a cut-over. It must arrive clearly ahead of the attack to be correct. Since the stop often ends with a double hit, it is not good to develop a habit of stopping unless you are clearly right.

Estimate your maximum lunging distance and then test your judgment. Can you barely hit the target from the starting position you chose?

As an opponent makes a simple attack, can you retreat just far enough so that the attack lands short by 4 or 5 inches?

By 1 or 2 inches?

Evaluation Questions

In the case of a double hit, the decision as to who is right rests with a director who may understandably have difficulty in accurately analyzing confusing actions.

The Time Thrust is similar to the stop thrust but is safer as the thrust is made with opposition which closes the line of attack. The time thrust is usually made against a compound attack. It should be timed so that the thrust is made during the feint of a one-two or a double. If the feint is to the sixth line, a simple extension with opposition should be made to the opponent's right shoulder. If the feint is to the fourth line, the extension should be made with opposition in eighth.

RIPOSTE

The riposte is a return attack made by a fencer who has parried an attack. The riposte may be simple or compound and may be made to any line. It may be made with a lunge if the opponent recovers to his guard position quickly, or it may be made by thrusting without a lunge if it is made quickly enough to arrive before the opponent has had time to recover.

An Immediate Riposte rebounds from the parry to score with a very fast direct thrust.

A Delayed Riposte is made after momentarily holding the parry, usually to riposte with a disengage or cut-over which is made as the opponent's arm returns to the guard position. The riposte may be made with compound attacks, but often these are too time-consuming so that, except to surprise the opponent by changing tactics, the simple ripostes tend to be the more successful.

A *Counter Riposte* may be made in just the same way by the fencer who successfully parries a riposte.

THE REMISE

The remise is an offensive action made by the attacker who fails to hit on his first attempt. It is a second action which places the point on the target without changing line and without withdrawing the arm. The remise may be made when the opponent parries but does not riposte, or when the riposte is delayed or composed. It must start before the final action of the riposte, if any, begins in order to maintain right of way.

When fencing a person who effectively uses the remise, immediate, simple ripostes are best because such a riposte has the legal right of way over a remise, whereas a delayed or compound riposte does not. On the other hand, when an opponent usually returns to the guard position after his attack is parried, the delayed or compound riposte may be more effective.

FENCING WITH THE ELECTRIC FOIL

Since fencing is a combat sport, it is natural that participants should seek competition with others once they have learned to use skills basic to fencing effectively. Most competitive fencing is now electrically scored, so a word should be said about fencing with the electrical foil which has been in general use since the 1955 World Championships.

The electric scoring apparatus is designed to determine hits made on a fencer with more accuracy than the average judge can assure. The fencer's personal equipment consists of an electric foil, a body cord, and a lamé vest which exactly covers the valid target and is worn over the regular fencing jacket.

The electric foil has a special point which is mounted on the end of the blade. The point is separated from its base by a spring which is depressed when a direct hit is made, causing the scoring apparatus to register a hit, valid or invalid. A thin wire connects with the point and runs down the length of the blade, where it is embedded in a groove on the top of the blade, to a plug on the inside of the guard. One end of the body cord plugs into the weapon and the other connects to the signalling apparatus.

35

The signalling machine is equipped with a buzzer, which gives an auditory signal for a hit and two lights for each fencer. Whenever a hit is made on the lamé vest, either a red or green light is lit, depending on which fencer scores. If a hit arrives off-target, it is indicated by a white light.

Anyone who intends to fence competitively should practice with an electric foil or with a dummy electric blade which feels like the electric weapon but is less expensive for everyday use.

The first electric weapons which were used were much heavier than the standard or nonelectric foil. Consequently, point control was seriously affected and for awhile it seemed that the methods of attack and defense would have to be modified. Weapons have been improved, however, so that while there is a difference in weight, the standard techniques are still correct. The difference is in the feel of the blade, which tends to be a little point heavy. The point tends to whip more which means that control is even more important than with the standard foil. A wide parry with the electric foil will travel farther and take longer to correct than it does when executed with a standard foil, so more precision is required.

Fencing has become increasingly mobile and increasingly fast so very complex attacks take too much time to execute. The stress now is on speed, accuracy, simplicity, and precise timing.

4

How to Practice

The person who wishes to excel in any sport must spend countless hours in practice. This holds particularly true for fencing. Improper practice can be detrimental if poor offensive and defensive actions are allowed to become habit patterns, so practice should always aim toward improving specific techniques. The fencer, whether beginning or experienced, must practice carefully and extensively in order to increase speed and accuracy of movements, endurance and strength, timing, and the ability to respond quickly and with versatility.

WARMING-UP

The values of warm-up exercises are to reduce the possibility of injury, to get a person mentally ready to perform, and perhaps to serve as practice for what is to follow. To reduce the possibility of injury, slow, long, deep lunges may serve as well as any other exercise as they will stretch the legs, groin, and torso areas which are used strenuously in fencing. Once the stretches have loosened these areas, lunges can be increased in speed so that the whole warm-up period can serve as practice for fencing.

IMPROVING SPEED AND ACCURACY

To improve speed and accuracy of movement so that instantaneous responses to sudden actions will be well executed, rather than large and uncontrolled, the fencer must concentrate on perfecting actions and repeat them again and again until perfect motions become automatic. Although you will often react to a sudden threat on a subcortical level, you will as often choose your actions, but you should have to decide only

On the wall, draw a 3 inch circle within each of the four areas of an imaginary target. On 20 consecutive full speed lunges can you hit a different circle each time?

Can you do this after starting with a retreat-advance-lunge?

Evaluation Questions

what movement to make, not how it will be executed. The HOW must be made automatic through repetition.

It has been found that speed and accuracy of a skill should be practiced together for the best improvement of these factors. Precision may be performed in slow motion in order to establish what is to be done, but once an action is understood it should be practiced at full but controlled speed if speed is to be developed.

The lunge, for instance, must be performed powerfully if a fencer is practicing to attack more effectively. Once you have lunged full-speed, stay in the lunge position long enough to make sure that all parts are correctly aligned. If they are not, correct the position and repeat again and again until you are satisfied that your full-speed lunge is well executed. When this point is reached, practice an immediate recovery from the full lunge to the guard position. You may also progress to the advance-lunge, recover, retreat, etc., which can be practiced in the same manner.

A padded target can be hung on a wall so that you can practice point control and proper thrusting along with footwork. If you lunge to hit a target, try to hit as near a specific spot as you can. Another valuable skill to be practiced at the same time is the ability to judge fencing distance accurately. From how far away can you lunge and hit? How far away should you be from the target to hit with an advance-lunge or ballestra attack?

Footwork can be practiced most effectively by yourself or with a capable person watching and correcting you; do not try to perfect your basic form as you fence when your mind must be occupied with many other things.

PRACTICING WITH ANOTHER FENCER

In order to make your practice time profitable, you should practice specific skills with another person. This can be interesting, challenging, and will more quickly improve your technique than free play.

Alternative Exercises—Any attack and defense can be practiced by having one person make attacks while the other parries. One fencer may, for instance, make disengage or one-two attacks while the other parries with only counter parries or only direct parries. Any techniques can be practiced in this way while the attacker tries to increase his speed and accuracy. The attacker must try to land each time in order to challenge the defender. The defender should occasionally allow an attack to land to make sure that the attack is well made. Trade off so that each works at attack and defense.

As soon as this simple exercise is mastered, progress by adding a riposte which may or may not be parried. More interest may later be stimulated by allowing the attacker to make any attack and the defender to make any defense and riposte. This should also be practiced with the advance-lunge as the defender retreats, then parries and ripostes with a lunge if necessary.

BOUTING PRACTICE

Only after drilling should you progress to actual bouting. Even bouting will be more advantageous if you try to use whatever skills you have previously practiced in a bout situation so that you can see what you still have to improve, if they fail, or so that you can gain confidence in your ability to execute various techniques successfully. As you bout you should try to analyze how each point which scored against you was made and what you could do to prevent it in the future. It is just as important to know exactly how you scored when you were successful in attacking. During actual competitions you will need to possess certain offensive actions in which you have full confidence, a necessary ingredient to successful fencing. It is important also to fence with as many different people as you can since you tend to become stereotyped when you fence with only one person whose every move you get to know. Of course you will profit most from working with fencers better than you, which means that the more skilled fencers have an obligation to the less skilled with whom they should spend some time but not an excessive amount, or such practice may work to the disadvantage of the better fencer. The highly skilled fencer may profit from working with beginners if he practices

> **With a partner, can you change engagement from four to six and vice versa?**
>
> **Can you catch the other blade before your partner can avoid yours three times out of ten? Five times? Seven times?**
>
> **How many times out of ten can you avoid his change?**

Evaluation Questions

for greater precision in spite of his opponent's larger motions. He may have more time to work on distance judgment or to experiment with new ideas. There is sometimes a tendency to make wide motions against a fencer who does the same, but this is always to be avoided. Fence your best, no matter with whom you are working.

Increasing Endurance—The strength-endurance factor, which is a requirement for today's fencer, can be increased in many ways. You can lunge 100 or more times a day, working until you are tired. This will increase endurance and also provide practice in lunging. Running will increase over-all stamina and to a degree leg strength. Running up stairs, preferably two stairs at a time, will increase endurance and will increase leg strength more than will straight running. You may also practice fencing for increasingly longer periods of time, working until you are fatigued in order to increase endurance.

Whatever method you choose, you must be in top physical condition to be a competitive fencer. College fencing tournaments frequently last for twelve or more hours during which time the contestants fence a bout, rest anywhere from two minutes to twenty minutes, fence again, etc. Strength and endurance are called for if participants are to keep fencing effectively over such an extended period. Because fencing is a very mobile game with many running attacks, or attacks in advance, it is extremely taxing, even for one hard-fought bout, and the fencer who is in poor physical condition will not be able to maintain his highest level of efficiency unless he is trained for continuous performance.

5

The Bout

The bout is much like a two-way conversation in that either person may take the initiative to which the other responds, and so on. Occasionally both may take the initiative at the same time, but usually it is a give and take situation.

The rules of fencing give precedence, or right-of-way, to the one who first seizes the initiative with an arm extension or with an attack. The attacker loses the right-of-way when the attack is parried or fails, or if the attacker withdraws his arm during an attack. Once the attack or feint is deflected, the defender has the right of way if he immediately seizes it to riposte. If he delays, neither party has right-of-way which may be retaken by either fencer, and so on.

When your technique has progressed sufficiently, you will want to test your ability against another fencer in a bout situation. Bouting is a

A crucial bout between two of the four finalists for the Men's Foil Championships during the 1964 Olympic Games at Tokyo.

true test of your speed, power, timing, ability to control your emotions and body, ability to analyze another fencer, and of your ingenuity. You are now completely on your own and you will win or lose according to how well you apply your knowledge. Your tactics will often call for split-second decisions which must be decisively carried out.

Whether you are engaged in informal bouting practice or in a tournament, you must try to score with the same determination or you will do a disservice to yourself and to your opponent. Neither of you will benefit from half-hearted attempts to attack or defend. In a practice bout, however, you are more free to experiment and to use attacks and defenses you have been practicing. In competitive fencing you must use actions in which you have gained confidence as you have practiced. The harder you have worked, and the more you have experimented in practice bouting, the more you will have to select from in a tournament situation.

The main problem in bouting with another person is "what" to do and "when" to do it. The main portion of this chapter is an attempt to answer these questions. In a contest between evenly matched fencers, the bout will go to the one who more effectively outthinks the other. You must always be aware of your own responses to probing actions made by your opponent. You should try not to respond to feints unless you choose to invite an attack in order to set up an action for yourself. You must avoid any repetitious actions such as a continual change of engagement in advance or patterns of beating without a definite plan in mind. Be aware of every move you make, know why you make it, and be aware of how your opponent reacts to what he learns about you.

TESTING FOR REACTIONS

The first thing you will probably do, once you face another fencer, is to test his responses. You must find out how fast he moves, how large or small his actions are, how he tends to react, what kind of traps he will fall into and what kind he will lay for you. If you fence against a person you know very well, you must still learn how he feels and how fast he is today.

There are a number of ways to discover what you want to know so that you can plan your tactics around what the other person is likely to do. This preliminary testing must be convincingly and suddenly done to draw a true response from an opponent who is probably trying the same things on you.

Responses to a Feint or False Attack—There are several responses you can draw from a feint or false attack:

1. A parry response, with or without a riposte, means that a one-two or double, depending on whether a direct or counter parry was used, will be a logical choice of attacks.

2. If a strong feint brings no response at all, your opponent is probably well controlled and will not parry until he is certain that you intend to hit with a direct attack. In this instance, try an explosive direct attack to score. If it succeeds, try the same thing again until it fails. If it was parried, how? You are again ready for a one-two or double, but your timing will be more difficult against a delayed parry. You will need a deep feint with a last minute evasion of the parry.

3. A retreat with or without a parry may indicate that an advance attack will be necessary for your proposed attack to reach. Plan an advance attack which will deceive any defensive attempts.

4. An extension into your feint tells you that you can expect your opponent to make stop thrusts. You can precede a straight thrust or disengage with a beat to either side of the blade to clearly gain right-of-way. You can also effectively make a second-intent attack in which you make a false attack, parry the stop, and continue to hit.

Responses to a Beat or Press—You can beat lightly on either side of the blade or press in the line of engagement to find your opponent's reactions. He may:

1. Make an answering beat or press, in which case you may beat or press and make a disengage or a one-two, timing the feint or disengage so that the answering beat or press will not find your blade and the opponent will be forced to go for a parry. If you are faster than he, a disengage may work, but if he parries well, a one-two will be better. You have set up a lateral movement with your preliminary action.

2. Make no response, which means that a strong beat-straight thrust may score. After being hit in this manner, the opponent will parry a strong feint of a straight thrust so that you can set up your deceptive attacks.

3. Attack as you beat or press. You can then "invite" him to attack by making a beat or press, then, since you are expecting the attack and will be ready, parry and riposte.

Responses to a Change of Engagement—With or without an advance, a change of engagement may reveal something about your opponent. He may:

1. Change his hand position to protect the line to which you have changed. You may change engagement, then make a disengage or

one-two as his hand moves to protect the line to which you made the change, again setting up a lateral response on the part of the other fencer. You can vary this action by making the attack to his low line.

2. Change engagement to the original line. You may change, then make a derobement, which is a disengage that avoids his change. If he parries this, avoid by disengaging again to the high or low line.

3. Make a disengage attack. Any time you change you must be ready for a possible derobement against yourself which you should parry, then riposte. The fact that you are prepared for this possible attack gives you an advantage. A counter parry may be more effective than a direct parry, as your opponent is more likely to try for a one-two than a double in the event of a parry.

4. Not respond at all, in which case you may change, feint a glide to force a response and deceive the parry. Caution is always necessary against someone who does not react to tentative maneuvers. He is probably planning to use these preliminary motions against you in the near future, so use variety and never set up a pattern of changing or beating unless you intend to invite an attack.

Responses to Simple Attacks or Beat Attacks—Often a sudden, explosive, unexpected attack can be enough of a surprise to be successful. If this works, try it until it fails, then you are ready for a composed attack to avoid whatever parry is used to block the attack.

VARYING YOUR DISTANCE

You should move about on the strip. If you freeze to one place on the strip you allow two things to happen: first, you allow your opponent too much time to get set for an attack; second, you tend to lessen your ability to move quickly and powerfully. As you move you can keep yourself ready to attack at all times. Any time you advance to within fencing distance, your opponent may make an attack which catches you slightly off-balance and moving into the attack. To avoid this, you should either extend your arm, beat-extend, or otherwise control the opponent's blade as you advance, but change what you do as you advance to lessen the likelihood of having your actions anticipated. Never just advance into a hit.

On the other hand, as you advance and retreat to varying distances you should try to draw your opponent a little too close. You must be completely alert so that you can attack at the exact instant he raises his toes to make an advance that will bring him within lunging distance, using an attack which, from previous preliminary movements, you are sure will land.

As a rule, you should retreat as you parry to add an extra margin of safety and to allow more time for your defense. If you retreat too far, however, you cannot riposte. By experience you will learn to retreat far enough for the attack to land just short, then a half or full lunge with the riposte will be sufficient to reach.

ATTACKS ON PREPARATION

The best time to attack is when your opponent is making motions preparatory to his attack, but before the actual attack begins. For instance, if by observation you learn that your opponent likes to make a beat or change in advance, you may make a disengage or a one-two which avoids his attempt to meet your blade as he steps in, or by making a bind, you may take the initiative from a feint. Absolute concentration and alertness are necessary if you are to time an attack on preparation successfully, but this is a very exciting way to fence since the split-second timing required tends to keep you on your toes to detect any movement of which you can take advantage..

BUILDING ATTACK SEQUENCES

The possibility of progressing from simple to complex actions has been alluded to in the beginning of this chapter, but perhaps this concept deserves special emphasis. To the degree that your opponent allows, you may lead him through a number of attacks in which you continue to build on his defensive responses to previous attacks.

You may first make a straight thrust, beat-straight thrust, disengage, or beat-disengage attack. Try to score and if you do, continue this attack until, in essence, you teach your opponent to parry the attack. You may advance, retreat, feint, or change engagement between attacks to divert your opponent's attention from your strategy. If you desire a direct parry to your direct attack, you are more likely to get such a response by attacking away from the other blade, rather than with opposition because a counter-parry is more difficult when it must be moderately wide. If your attack fails because your opponent, now convinced that you will continue to make simple attacks, parries with a direct parry, you will follow this up with a one-two attack. The one-two may be used, interspersed with diverting byplay, until it is parried with a second parry, at which time you may make the one-two by making the last action to the low line.

How might fencer B safely attack fencer A?

If your opponent switches to counter parries, you may similarly progress to double attacks.

Another example of a sequence of attacks begins with a cut-over from the line of four to six. If you are engaged in four you may make a simple cut-over or a press, cut-over which may open the sixth line further if your opponent responds to the press with pressure of his own. If you begin in six, you may change engagement to four and make the cut-over as your opponent starts to close his fourth line. This is an effective attack and should land. When this is parried by a direct parry of six, you may, on the next attack feint a cut-over, avoid the sixth parry to disengage low to eighth. When this attack is parried you may progress to a feint of a cut-over to eighth, disengage to sixth.

There will be other byplay between attacks while you keep the offensive by controlling the blade, changing distance, or going to the defense yourself. The time you pick to attack is important. The distance must be right, and your opponent must be caught as he relaxes a little or as his attention wanders momentarily. You must surprise him.

THE LEFT-HANDED FENCER

Those who are left-handed may have a psychological advantage over some fencers, and they will have a technical advantage over those who are unfamiliar with left-handed fencers. Right-handed fencers should fence with left-handers often to familiarize themselves with the differences which exist between left and right-handed fencing.

Diagram E:

ATTACKING

The left-handers must develop a strong defense in the outside lines, since this will be their most vulnerable area. When fencing a right-hander, they will be in six, a weaker line, when the right-hander is in the stronger line of four, and vice versa. A strong parry of six, counter-six, and eight are important to both left- and right-handed fencers when they work with each other.

Very few inside attacks will succeed here, but a one-two to the inside, then outside high or low line, is an effective attack against either fencer. Accuracy is important here since the outside lines are smaller than those on the inside, but they are more accessible.

Attacks on preparation may be made if either fencer insists on engaging either in six or four. The attacker may change to the non-favored line and make a derobement as the other fencer changes back to his preferred line.

SUGGESTED COUNTERS TO COMMON SYSTEMS OF FENCING

There are many possible ways of dealing with various strategies. The important thing is to recognize a style for what it is and plan to use this knowledge to your own advantage. The following represent possible means of solving some common problems which may be encountered:

1. Against a fencer who makes many stop or time thrusts, you may succeed with second-intent attacks.
2. Against an opponent who refuses to attack but who has a deadly parry-riposte, you may also be successful with a second-thrust attack

which will bring about the desired attack for your parry and counter riposte.

3. Against a fencer who is always out of reach, you may make a ballestra attack, you may redouble to pursue the opponent, or you may retreat yourself to attack as he advances into distance.

4. Against a fencer who wants to control your blade and who makes many beat-attacks, you may fence with absence of the blade. If you take a low line guard, your opponent will be frustrated in his attempt to take your blade. If he goes to low line to find your blade, a fairly large action, you may take the initiative with a derobement to the high line. You may pretend to give him your blade and disengage as he moves to find your blade.

5. Against a person who always makes an advance-attack or ballestra, you may upset the distance by occasionally holding your ground rather than retreating. Since this moving attack is calculated to reach a retreating defender, by holding your ground he will not have reached the final phase of his attack by the time the distance to your target is closed, and his point will probably miss as he is not yet ready for the final thrust. The riposte after your parry is not difficult as you know what the distance will be and can thrust accordingly.

6. Against bent arm simple attacks, a time thrust is effective. Against a poor compound attack, a stop thrust made before the final action begins can take the right of way.

HINTS FOR THE DEFENSE

Control is the watchword for the defender. You should concentrate your gaze on the center of the target. You should not try to watch the point as it moves too wide and too fast for the eye to follow. Neither should you try to follow movements of the hand with your eyes. If you watch a central point on the target, you will be able to see all that develops with your peripheral vision. You will see any shoulder movements which may telegraph an attack, you will see where the hand moves, and you will be able to see foot movements without having to follow all of these movements with your eye.

Try not to parry feints but only the real attacks. The ability to tell a feint from an attack is acquired with experience, but the beginner can refuse to parry until the lunge actually develops. By delaying the parry, you give fewer clues to your opponent and you make compound attacks difficult to time. Ideally, you should parry just before the point lands, which takes a good eye, control and precision in the parry.

6

The Language
and Lore of Fencing

Most fencing terms are descriptive of the actions to which they refer. Many of the terms in common usage in this country reflect the French or Italian origins of fencing, and although much of our terminology has been adapted or translated to English, many works are European. All international fencing championships are conducted in French, which is the international language of fencing, so the French influence predominates in terminology. Any real student of fencing should become familiar with the fencing vocabulary.

Most forms of attack and defense were first introduced many years ago by European fencing masters, many of whom sold their secret attacks or defenses to duellists who were willing to pay dearly for them. Usually the student was instructed behind closed doors and was sworn to secrecy so that these tricks would not become general knowledge, which would cause them to be less effective. Today's fencing is made up largely of refinements and modifications of these old actions which, through the years, have proven themselves to be the best means of attack and defense.

Abstain—a judge may "abstain" or decline to vote if he was unable to see whether or not a point was made.

Absence of the blade—when the blades are not engaged.

Advance—to move forward in the guard position.

A.F.L.A.—Amateur Fencers League of America. This is the governing body of amateur fencing in the United States. It establishes rules and regulations and selects teams for international competitions. Founded in 1891, the A.F.L.A. is affiliated with the Fédération International d'Escrime.

Attack—an initial attempt to hit the opponent.

Attack on preparation—an attack which is made as the opponent makes a beat, change, feint, or advance in preparation for his attack. This attack must begin before the opponent's attack actually begins.

Attack on the blade—an action, such as a beat, press or bind, which removes the opponent's blade from line to clear the way for an attack.

Ballestra—a jump-lunge attack. This term suggests the historic link between fencing and the formal ballet, which is said to have been influenced by the basic fencing positions.

Barrage—a fence-off of a tie between two or more fencers.

Beat—a sharp tap against the opponent's blade to clear the way for an offensive action.

Bind (Liément)—an action which removes a threatening blade by "binding" it, or carrying it from high line to the opposite low line by crossing the blade over the opponent's blade to hit in the low line with opposition. If the bind is executed vigorously enough, it may be used to disarm an opponent. Disarming an opponent, however, is no longer advantageous since action stops whenever a weapon is dropped. In the days of duelling and of early fencing, this was a valuable trick to master. Today it is a useful action, but no attempt is made to actually disarm a fencer by this means.

Call—a signal to stop the bout. If a fencer wishes to stop during a bout without danger of being hit, he may "call" to the director to stop the bout by quickly stamping the forward foot two times.

Change of engagement—the act of going from one line to engage the blade in another.

Closed line—a line which is protected by the blade and arm.

Compound attack—any attack consisting of two or more actions. It may also be called a composed attack.

Corps-á-corps (clinch)—literally body-to-body, in which there is body contact or a closing of the guards so that normal fencing actions become impossible.

Coulé (glide)—a preparatory action which is made by gliding along the side of the opponent's blade.

—*Counterattack*—a stop thrust or time thrust in which the time is taken from the attacker by an arm extension before the final action of the original attack.

Counter-parry—a circular parry which is made by parrying in the side opposite the one to which an atack is made.

Counter-riposte—an offensive action which follows the successful parry of a riposte.

Counter-time—a second intention attack.

Coupé (cut-over)—a simple attack which is made by lifting the blade over the opponent's blade to hit in the opposite line.

Croise—an action, similar to the bind, in which the blade crosses over a menacing blade to carry it from a high line to the low line on the same side. This action is used in preference to a bind as a time-thrust, as it is a quicker action since it does not draw the other blade across the target.

Derobement (deception)—an evasion of the opponent's attempt to engage or beat the blade.

Direct—indicates that an attack or parry is made without changing lines.

Disengage—a simple attack which is made by leaving the line of engagement to hit in another.

Double—a compound attack in which the attacker feints a disengage and deceives a counter-parry. This may be described as a "corkscrew" attack.

Engagement—the contact of two opposing blades.

Envelopment—a double bind which envelops the opposing, menacing blade in a motion which carries it in a complete circle to land in the line of the original engagement.

False attack—a lunge which is made to draw a response but without intent to land.

Feint—a pretended attack which is made by a menacing extension of the foil arm. It is made preparatory to an attack in order to draw a response.

Fencing time—the time required to make one simple fencing action. This time will vary according to the speed of the fencers in question.

F.I.E.—Fédération Internationale d'Escrime. The governing body of all international fencing tournaments. This organization was founded in Europe in the latter part of the nineteenth century, at which time some rules were set up to govern tournaments.

Flèche—a running attack. The literal translation from French is "arrow" which describes this as a swift, flying attack.

Foible—the flexible, or point half of the blade.

Forte—the strong half of the blade which extends from the guard.

Lines—the four theoretical areas of the target: upper inside and outside; and lower inside and outside.

Lunge—an extension of the guard position in order to reach the opponent. The lunge was introduced during the last of the sixteenth century as a new secret form of attack.

Mask—the protective wire helmet which is worn on the head. The first masks were made from sheet metal with eye slits cut into them. These were never in wide use as they were uncomfortable, and the eye became vulnerable to hits as the metal allowed the point to slide to the eye slits thus making these masks very dangerous. Some right-of-way conventions of fencing stem from the pre-mask days when, for instance, it was considered wrong to riposte until the opponent had recovered from his lunge because to do so would be extremely hazardous. The first wire masks were used in about 1800.

Off-target hit—a point hit which does not land on the valid target. This term is now preferred to the term "foul."

On guard—the basic "ready" fencing position.

One-two—a compound attack which consists of: feint a disengage, disengage to deceive a direct parry.

Parry—a defensive action which deflects the attacker's blade.

Pass—when the foil point grazes the target, rather than hitting squarely.

Piste (strip)—from the French word meaning "path." This is the fencing area which may be said to resemble a path or strip because of its long narrow shape.

Phrase or phrase d'armes—a period of continuous fencing which may consist of many actions by one or both fencers. When there is any break in play a phrase ends.

Pommel—the metal part at the end of the handle which serves to fasten the parts of the foil together and also acts as a counterweight to the blade, thereby making the foil a balanced weapon.

President (director)—the individual who presides over a fencing meet.

Pressure—a preliminary motion made by applying a slight pressure against the opponent's blade to cause a reaction which will open the way for an attack.

Prise-de-fer—a taking of the blade of the opponent. This refers to blade contact.

Redoublement—a new offensive action made against a fencer who defends without riposting.

Remise—an immediate continuation of an attack which was parried or which fell short. It is made without withdrawing the arm, usually while in a lunge.

Reprise—a new attack made after returning to the guard position.

Right-of-way—the right to attack which goes to the fencer who first extends his arm, first initiates an attack, or parries an attack.

Riposte—an answering attack, made by a fencer after he successfully defends himself.

⎯ *Second intention attack*—a false attack intended to draw a parry-riposte which the original attacker then parries so he can hit on a counter-riposte, which means that he intends to hit on his second attack.

Semicircular parry—a parry from high to low line or vice versa, so called because the point travels in an arc to make the parry.

Simple attack—an attack consisting of just one motion. There are three simple attacks: straight thrust, disengage, and cut-over.

Stop thrust—a counterattack made by extending into a poorly executed attack. In order to be valid a stop must arrive before the final motion of the attack begins.

Straight thrust—a direct, simple attack. A lunge to hit without changing the line of engagement.

Strip (piste)—the field of play. The strip is usually made of rubber so that fencers will not slip as they move. In electric fencing meets the strip may be covered with wire mesh which grounds any hits to the floor which would otherwise register as an off-target hit.

Thrust—the action of hitting with an extended arm. The point is placed on the target with the action of the fingers to make a firm thrust.

Time-thrust—a counterattack which is made in opposition of the opponent's blade, thereby constituting a parry and riposte in one motion.

Touch—a valid point hit against the opponent.

Valid touch—a point hit which lands on the target area without having first landed off-target.

7

Rules of Fencing

The Amateur Fencers League of America publishes the rules which govern fencing tournaments in this counrty. These rules correlate closely with the rules which are set forth by the Federation Internationale d'Escrime, the governing body of international fencing. The F.I.E. first published technical rules of fencing in 1914 for use at the Olympic Games. These rules have been modified and revised periodically. In 1958 they were revised and renamed "Rules for Competition."[1]

The rules which are presented in this chapter are taken from the 1965 edition of the A.F.L.A. Manual with the permission of Jose R. de Capriles, editor of the Manual. The rules discussed here are not complete. They are intended to serve as an overview and to provide enough information for informal bouting or for classroom tournaments. If a fencer intends to enter intercollegiate or A.F.L.A. competitions, he should read the official Rules Manual. The Manual is sent to each member of the A.F.L.A. and is paid for out of his dues, or it can be purchased for $3.00 from:

> Amateur Fencers League of America, Inc.
> 33 62nd Street
> West New York, N.J. 07093.

FIELD OF PLAY

The strip, or piste, may have a wood, rubber, linoleum, cork, or plastic surface. The strip is from 1m80 to 2m (5 ft. 11 in. to 6 ft. 7 in.) wide and 12m (39 ft. 4 in.) long. Seven lines should be drawn across the width of

---

[1]Fencing Rules & Manual, Amateur Fencers League of America, Heffernan Press Inc., Mass. 1965. p. 13.

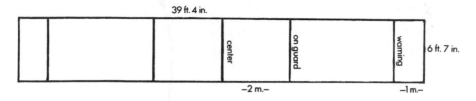

Figure 28—The Strip

the strip: one center line; two on guard lines, one drawn 2m (6 ft. 7 in.) from each side of the center line; two end lines at the rear limit of the strip; two warning lines marked 1m (3 ft. 3 in.) in front of the end lines.

CLOTHING

Fencers are responsible for their own safety. They must wear an all white uniform which provides for the maximum safety possible without sacrificing freedom of movement.

The jacket must overlap the trousers at the waist by at least 4 in. in the guard position. Women, especially in electrically scored events, are required to wear rigid breast protectors in addition to the padded jacket.

Men and women are required to wear trousers which fasten below the knee.

The gauntlet of the glove must cover about half of the forearm to prevent the opponent's blade from entering the jacket sleeve.

OFFICIALS

The Director or President—The Director is completely in charge of the bout over which he presides. His duties are: to stop and start the bout; to control the equipment in the sense that any unsafe or illegal clothing or equipment may not be allowed; to supervise the judges, timers, scorers, etc.; to maintain order; to penalize for faults; to award hits.

The Jury—If a tournament is fenced with standard (non-electric) weapons, the jury consists of four judges. If the event is electrically scored, the jury consists of two Ground-Judges when there is no metallic strip.

Duties of the Judges—Two judges stand on each side of the Director, one on each side of the strip, and slightly behind the fencers. The judges watch the fencer who is furtherest from them, so the two judges on the Director's right watch the fencer on the Director's left, and vice versa.

55

Judges watch for hits which land anywhere on the fencer. When a point lands, the judge must immediately signal the Director by raising his hand, at which time the Director must call "halt."

METHOD OF DETERMINING HITS. The Director must briefly reconstruct the actions of the last phrase, asking the appropriate judges in the course of the analysis of play, whether a hit was made.

A judge may respond by saying: "yes," which means a valid hit was made; "off-target," which means a hit landed but was not valid; "no"; or "I abstain," which means that the judge did not see the action, which may have been blocked from his vision by one or both fencers, and declines to vote.

The Director adds his vote last, at which time he adds the votes as follows: one point for the vote of each judge; one and a half points for his own vote; and no points for an abstention. A simple majority decides how the point will be awarded. If two judges on one side agree that a point was valid, off-target, or did not land, their decision must stand, even if the Director does not agree, because their two points outweigh the Director's one and a half points.

If, on the other hand, one judge says "no" and one says "yes" or, "off-target," the Director will have the deciding vote.

If one judge says "yes," "off-target," or "no," and the other abstains, the Director may overrule that one judge if he does not agree with him.

If one judge answers "yes" or "off-target" and the other answers "no," and if the director must abstain, no point is awarded, but no subsequent action may be awarded against the fencer who might have landed a hit. If the fencer who made the doubtful hit then makes a definite hit without a hit having landed against him, the hit must be awarded.

The jury decides materiality of hits. Once materiality has been decided upon, the Director alone decides on the validity of a hit. In the event that two hits arrive, the Director must determine to which, if either, fencer to award the point.

Ground-Judges—When a meet is electrically scored, but not fenced on a metal strip, two Ground-Judges are needed. One Judge stands on each side of the Director at opposite ends of the strip and observes all action to determine whether a hit, which registers as an off-target hit, was made on the floor.

Scorer—The scorer marks points against the fencer who the Director declares was hit. The scorer marks the hit and announces the name and score of the person just hit, then the score of the other fencer. The scorer also calls fencers to the strip to fence, and announces "on deck" bouts so that the next two who will fence will be ready when their turn comes and no time will be lost in starting the next bout.

Timer—In an official meet a time limit is set on bouts. The time is kept by a stop watch of actual fencing time only. Time is "in" from the Director's command of "fence" to that of "halt." The timer signals the Director, who must stop the bout and warn the fencers, one minute before time is up.

CONVENTIONS OF FOIL FENCING

Hitting—The foil is a thrusting weapon only and offensive actions must be made with the point which must distinctly reach the target in order to be counted as a hit.

Figure 29—The Target is Defined by the Metallic Vest Which is worn During Electrically Scored Tournaments.

Target—The valid target for men and women, is the torso from the collar to a horizontal line which joins the tops of the hip bones across the back, and to the groin line in front. The arms, from the shoulder seams outward, are excluded. The bib of the mask is also excluded.

Off-Target Hits—When a point hit is made on any part of the body other than the target, it is not a valid hit, but stops all action and no subsequent hit may be counted.

Length of a Bout—Men fence until one person has been hit five times and women four times. If it is a timed meet, the time limits are: six minutes of actual fencing time for men, and five minutes for women. Fencers may ask the score during a bout, but they may not ask how much time remains. If the time limit expires before a bout is completed, the score will be advanced for each fencer to meet the required number of points for a bout. In a men's five point bout, for instance, if time runs out when the score is 3-1, two points will be added to each score to make the official score 5-3. If a bout is tied at the end of the fencing period, the score will be advanced to 4-4 and fencers will continue, regardless of time, until the final point is won. Fencers receive a verbal warning from the Director when one minute of time remains.

Combat

METHOD OF FENCING. Competitors may fence in any manner as long as they do not violate the basic rules of fencing.

The rules require that all bouts be fenced in a courteous, sportsmanlike way with no violent actions which may be considered dangerous.

HANDLING THE WEAPON. The foil may be used with one hand only. A fencer may not switch hands during a bout unless the Director gives special permission as the result of a wound.

COMING ON GUARD. The fencer whose name is called first should come on guard on the Director's right, unless the first person called is a left-handed fencer.

The fencers must start in the center of the width of the strip, with both feet behind the on-guard line which is 6 ft. 7 in. from the center line.

At the command "On Guard," the fencers come to a guard position, after which the Director next asks, "Are you ready?" When both fencers reply in the affirmative, the Director begins the bout with the command "fence."

BEGINNING, STOPPING AND RESTARTING THE BOUT. At the command "fence," time is in and either fencer may initiate the offensive. Once play begins the contestants may stop only at their own risk until the bout is officially stopped by the command "halt."

Only the Director may halt the bout, except for reasons of safety, when a judge may halt the bout. If, for instance, a judge sees an injury or a broken blade, he may stop the bout.

The Director stops the bout when a hit, valid or off-target, is made; when a fencer steps off of the strip with both feet; anytime a corps-á-corps or any other irregular play exists; whenever a judge raises his hand; or when, in his opinion, the bout should be stopped for any reason.

FENCING AT CLOSE QUARTERS. This is allowed so long as the fencers are able to use their weapons correctly and the Director can follow the action.

DISPLACING THE TARGET AND REVERSING POSITIONS. Displacing the target, ducking, or turning is allowed. Reversing of position on the strip, however, is not allowed, and if this should occur, fencers will be halted and put on guard in their original positions.

GROUND GAINED OR LOST. When the bout is halted each fencer must, if necessary, retreat equally in order to attain fencing distance with the following exceptions: when a valid hit is scored, fencers will be put on guard equidistant from the center of the strip as they were at the beginning of the bout; when a bout stops because of a corps-à-corps or flèche, only the fencer who caused the clinch must give ground; a competitor shall not be put on guard behind the warning line if he has not been previously warned; a fencer who was behind the warning line when the bout was stopped shall not have to give ground.

STEPPING OFF OF THE STRIP. Whenever a fencer steps off of the strip with both feet the Director must immediately call "halt." If a fencer is hit as he steps off by an action that was in motion as he stepped off the strip, the hit must be awarded. Any hit made by a fencer who has stepped off of the strip must be annulled.

Rear Limits of the Strip. When the rear foot reaches the warning line, the Director must halt the bout to warn the fencer that he is nearing the end line. This warning will be repeated after the warned fencer advances so that his front foot reaches his on guard line and retreats again to the warning line.

If a fencer, after a warning, crosses the rear line with both feet, a point is scored against him. If a fencer crosses the end line without having been warned, he will be put on guard at the warning line with no penalty.

Lateral Boundaries. When a fencer crosses a side line with both feet he is penalized 1m (3 ft. 3 in.). If this penalty places a fencer over the end line with both feet, after having been warned at the warning line, a hit will be awarded against him.

If a fencer crosses a boundary to avoid being hit, he will be warned. The second time this occurs during the same bout, a hit will be awarded against him. If a fencer accidentally leaves the strip, there is no penalty.

CORPS-À-CORPS AND FLÈCHE ATTACKS. When a fencer systematically causes a corps-à-corps, even without violence, he must be first warned, and then penalized one hit for each repetition during the same bout.

OFFICIATING TECHNIQUES

In most fencing tournaments fencers are expected to be willing and able to assist with the officiating. Directors are, for the most part, amateur fencers who gladly give their time in the interests of fencing. It is desirable therefore, that all fencers learn to officiate in any capacity so that they may assist in the running of meets and so that they may better understand and appreciate all aspects of the sport.

It takes experience to become a good Director or Judge. These tasks require the entire attention of officials involved if they are to accurately see and explain what occurs during a bout. The entire climate of a tournament is affected by the attitude and ability of the Director and his jury who may either inspire confidence and establish a high level of efficiency, or may allow indecision and poor sportsmanship to lower the standards and morale of fencers and spectators alike.

Directing Techniques. The Director is a vital part of a tournament. He is responsible for and has authority over actions of fencers and spectators alike. He sets the standards and overall climate of the meet.

The Director must know the rules, but in case he is challenged, or if an unusual situation arises, a rule book should be available at every fencing meet.

The Director's voice should be clear and authoritative so that the commands of "fence" and "halt" may be clearly heard by fencers and the timer.

Starting the Bout—The Director must see that fencers and officials are all in place before beginning. As soon as they are in place he asks, "are you ready?" When the fencers reply in the affirmative, he commands, "fence."

Directing With a Jury—The Director allows play to continue until a point lands, any irregular fencing occurs, or for any reason he feels it should be stopped.

A Director can upset fencers by calling "halt" too often and without reason. As long as no point lands and fencing is not too confusing to follow, competitors should be allowed to continue, but whenever there is cause the bout should be halted immediately. If several actions continue after a point lands, the job of analyzing play is made more difficult, so the call to "halt" must be quickly made once a point does arrive.

When action stops because of a possible hit the Director should quickly give a résumé of the last phrase. The Director should remember that he is there to run a bout efficiently with a minimum of delays, not to put on an exhibition of his knowledge or overshadow the fencing with his performance. He is there to facilitate fencing only and lengthy explanations of every detail of the bout may unduly delay the game.

After a brief description of the last phrase, the Director should question the judges as to materiality of hits. He will follow the right-of-way sequence and determine whether the first attack landed. If it did, and the right-of-way was clear, a point is awarded and no further questions need be asked. If the attack failed, he must find out which, if any, subsequent action landed and award hits according to his findings.

The Director should always give his own opinion of materiality last so that he in no way influences the responses made by the judges. He should not lead the judges with such questions as, "did you see the point land on the hand?", or "do you agree that the point missed?" It would be better to task, "did the attack land?"; a simple statement which does not suggest how the judge should answer.

Validity. The Director alone is responsible for determining validity in case both fencers are hit. He may also see points land, but first he must know the sequence of action. If two hits arrive at about the same time, the Director must decide which fencer had the right-of-way, and if he cannot, he should declare a double touch in which case no hit will be awarded.

In order to follow the action of a bout, the Director should stand far enough from the fencers to get a comprehensive view of both fencers so that he can see all that occurs without having to turn his head from side to side as the action develops. The Director should try to stand in the center of the field of play, which means that he will have to move with the fencers. When a "halt" is called and no touch is awarded, the Director must indicate the center of the field of play so fencers will properly position themselves when they are ready to resume action. Besides affording a good view of the action, this central position simplifies the task of indicating the center of the field of play, and keeps the director from obscuring the action from the judges.

Judging Techniques—The judges watch materiality of hits against the fencer who is furthest from them. They are to assist the Director and are not to in any way try to dominate or delay the fencing.

The judges must move with the action so that they maintain their position just behind the nearest fencer and to the side of the strip. In this position they will not obstruct the view of the Director or get in the way of the fencers, yet at least one of the two judges on each end of the strip will have a clear view of what happens. While the judges are not responsible for knowing who has the right-of-way, they must know how many actions were made against the fencer they are watching so that they will know which attempt touched, when there is a series of

These fencers have made valid touches at about the same time. Under what circumstances would you declare fencer A hit?

Fencer B hit?

Evaluation Questions

SIMULTANEOUS TOUCHES

actions. The judges can profit from counting actions as they occur so they can clearly say whether it was the first, second, or fourth action which landed.

The judge must instantly raise his hand when he sees a point land, on or off-target. If he hesitates it will be harder to decide which action landed and time will be lost, so the hand must be raised quickly, and it must be raised high enough to be clearly seen out of the corner of the Director's eye. Conversely, he must not raise his hand unless he sees something land. Nothing is more annoying to a fencer who has planned a series of actions to lead to a hit, than to have a judge stop his action by raising his hand only to say, "no, I guess nothing really happened," or "I'm not sure."

When the Director asks a judge whether an action landed or not, he does not want a lengthy description of where and how the point went. The judge's response should be: "yes"; "off-target"; "no"; or "abstain." A good judge abstains when he does not see whether a point landed, but it may be a weak, indecisive answer from a judge who is afraid to express an opinion for fear of being wrong. The judge tells what he saw independently of what another judge says. He should not be influenced by comments or gestures from fencers or spectators. He must be sure of himself and answer to the best of his ability at all times, not just take the easy way out by refusing to vote.

Directing With Electrical Apparatus—The duties of the Director are the same whether a meet is electrically scored or not, but the means of deciding touches is different. When there are no judges to assume partial responsibility the Director's task is perhaps even more demanding. Although the machine alone can determine if a point has been made, the

Diagram F:

SIMULTANEOUS
TOUCHES

Director must know all of the action which takes place and he must also watch the scoring box so he will see when a light goes on.

His first task, at the start of each bout, is to see that all equipment is working properly before fencing begins, even though fencers are responsible for their own personal equipment. If a foil is not registering properly or there are any tears in an electric vest, he must see that they· are repaired or replaced.

POSITION. The Director should stand so that he can see the scoring lights at all times as well as the action. This means that, except when fencers are in the center of the strip, the Director will stand at one end of the action or the other as necessary to see both the fencers and the lights. In the event that lights for each fencer go on, the Director must still know the right-of-way to decide to whom to award a point.

How to Read the Lights. There are two lights for each fencer: a white light and a colored light. The bout must be halted whenever a light and the buzzer go on. No touch may be awarded unless it has been registered by the machine.

If only a white light turns on, an off-target hit has been made against the fencer on whose side the light appears. If only a colored light registers, a valid touch was made against the fencer on whose side the light appears.

If both a colored and white light register on the same side, an off-target hit was made before a valid hit and no point may be awarded.

If lights appear on both sides, the Director must determine the validity and award the hit accordingly or declare a double hit with no score.

Only the apparatus may determine materiality of a hit. If however, the Director suspects that a hit was indicated when none occurred, that

63

point may be disregarded if the electric equipment is found to be faulty. No hit may be awarded unless it registers, even if a fault in the equipment is found.

General Rules for Determining the Validity of Hits. The Director alone decides on validity of hits in the event that both fencers are touched. The fencers may not question the Director's judgment as to what occurred, but they may question his application of rules in view of what the judges and Director say took place. The following are the basic right of way rules which must be used in determining validity:[2]

Article 233

Observance of the fencing phrase.

1. All correctly executed attacks must be parried or completely avoided and the phrase must be followed through. In order to judge as to the correctness of an attack the following points must be considered:
   a. If the attack is initiated when the opponent has his "point in line" (i.e., "with the arm straight and point threatening the target") the attacker must first deflect his opponent's weapon.
   b. If the attack is commenced when the opponent's blade is not in line, the attack may be completed either direct, or by one disengagement or by a cut-over, or else be preceded by successful feints which oblige the opponent to form a parry.
   c. If, when attempting to find the opponent's blade to deflect it, the blade is not found, the right of attack passes to the opponent.

234 2. The parry gives the right to riposte: the simple riposte may be direct or indirect, but to annul any subsequent action by the attacker, it must be executed immediately, without indecision or delay.

235 3. If a composed attack is made and the opponent finds the blade during one of the feints, he has the right to riposte.

236 4. When composed attacks are made, the opponent has the right to stop hit; but to be valid the stop hit must precede the conclusion of the attack by an interval of fencing time; that is to say that the stop hit must arrive before the attacker has begun the final movement of the attack.

Judging of hits.

237 In applying the basic conventions of foil fencing, the President should judge as follows:

---

[2]Fencing Rules & Manual, Amateur Fencers League of America, Heffernan Press Inc., Mass. 1965. pp. 44-46. Used by permission of Jose R. de Capriles, Editor.

When, during a phrase, both fencers are hit simultaneously, there is either a simultaneous action or a double hit.

The first of these conditions is due to simultaneous conception and execution of an attack by both fencers even if one of them has been hit off the target.

The double hit on the other hand, is the result of a faulty action on the part of one of the fencers.

Therefore, when there is not a period of fencing time between the hits:

1. The fencer who is attacked is alone counted as hit:
   - a. If he makes a stop hit on his opponent's simple attack;
   - b. If, instead of parrying, he attempts to avoid the hit and does not succeed in so doing;
   - c. If, after a parry is effected, he makes a momentary pause which gives his opponent the right to re-attack;
   - d. If, during a composed attack, he makes a stop hit without being in time;
   - e. If, having his "point in line" and being subjected to a beat or a prise-de-fer which deflects his blade, he attacks or places his point in line again instead of parrying a direct thrust made by his opponent.

2. The fencer who attacks is alone counted as hit:
   - a. If he initiates his attack when his opponent has his point in line without deflecting the opponent's weapon;
   - b. If he attempts to find the blade, does not succeed and continues the attack;
   - c. If, during a composed attack, he allows his opponent to find the blade, and continues the attack while his opponent ripostes immediately;
   - d. If, during a composed attack, he makes a momentary pause, during which time the opponent makes a stop hit while the attacker continues his attack;
   - e. If, during a composed attack, he is stopped in time before he begins his final movement; (A one-two, double, or any similar action is considered as a single movement attack when properly executed.)
   - f. If he makes a hit by a remise, redoublement or reprise on his opponent's parry, which has been followed by a riposte which is immediate, simple, and executed in one period of fencing time without withdrawing the arm.

Unwritten
Laws of Fencing

During the so-called age of chivalry in the sixteenth century, the popularity of duelling went hand-in-hand with the development of fencing into a fine art as fencers realized the necessity of improving their skill. The sword become a gentleman's badge which was worn only by nobility who practiced diligently to become adept in its use. Noble women also studied fencing and there are recorded instances of duels between women. The courtesies of fencing practice and of duelling were elaborate and precise as was in keeping with the elevated station of the participants.

Fencing etiquette today reflects the general spirit which prevailed in the heyday of fencing. Fencing is still a sport for ladies and gentlemen as far as behavior is concerned and the accepted standards of fencing conduct are universal.

Until the early twentieth century fencing form and sportsmanship were considered as important as scoring. Tournaments were judged on the basis of form, much as gymnastics is judged today; the manner in which one made an attack or defense was as important as whether or not it succeeded.

Fencers were required to acknowledge hits against themselves and were penalized if judges saw a hit which was not admitted.

Today the criterion on which a fencer is judged is the more realistic one of whether or not a point lands, but poor sportsmanship and unnecessary roughness may still cost a fencer points.

There are not many rules of conduct, but the comprehensive written and unwritten laws of etiquette are taught and adhered to in all reputable fencing centers throughout the world.

CONDUCT OF THE FENCERS

Fencers always salute each other before putting on their masks. In a tournament the director, the audience, and then the opponent are quickly saluted. At the end of a bout fencers remove their masks and then shake ungloved hands.

Informal Bouting—During informal play in the classroom or Salle d'Armes, fencers are expected to acknowledge all touches against themselves, whether valid or off-target. Fencers do not claim touches against the opponent, but a fencer may refuse to accept a point if, in his opinion, it was not a good hit.

Tournament Fencing—In a tournament a fencer may acknowledge a touch against himself, but usually fencers remain silent when they are hit. A fencer never challenges the opinion of the judge or the director as to what occurred.

It is considered bad manners to attempt to influence a judge in any way, directly or indirectly. A fencer should not, for instance, rub his arm or leg to convince a judge that a hit was off-target, or pretend to straighten his blade after an attack to indicate that a hit should be called. Nor should a fencer stop fencing and obviously wait for his judge to indicate that his attack was successful. If a fencer does stop to wait for a call he may be hit.

If a fencer turns and walks away after an attack it is proper for his opponent to hit him on the back. A fencer stops only at his own risk. If a fencer hits cleanly and correctly, the touch will be called. If sometimes a fencer disagrees with a decision, he must realize that the jury is often better able to judge what happened than he is, and that the few inevitable mistakes which occur in all probability will be made equally in favor of each contestant. The best fencers rely on ability, not dramatics, in order to win.

A fencer may politely ask for an explanation of a decision, but he may not challenge as to whether a hit landed or when.

Tension often mounts as fencers wait for the proper moment to attack. Their concentration is intense and to competitors each point is of the utmost importance, so occasional outbursts do occur; but a fencer must not violate the basic rules of courtesy and good sportsmanship.

CONDUCT OF THE SPECTATORS

The audience at a fencing tournament acts similarly to that at a tennis match. Spectators must not try to influence officials or instruct contestants in any way, although they may applaud a well-executed attack. For the most part, quiet is necessary so that fencers can hear commands of the Director and so that their attention will not be unduly diverted by excessive noise. The Director can demand silence or may, in extreme situations, exclude members of the audience who do not conform to these standards.

9

Selection of Equipment

Fencing equipment is relatively inexpensive and with care should last for many years. Although many schools furnish the clothing and equipment needed, anyone who seriously wants to fence should invest in his or her own personal equipment. All necessary clothing and equipment can be purchased from most fencing Salles or Clubs. Any school or fencing group can advise you regarding your fencing needs.

JACKET

This is a vital part of your uniform and should be of good quality. Any manufacturer of fencing clothing must adhere to the minimum safety standards which are required by the rules. Half-jackets or plastrons can be purchased at less cost than a full jacket, but since these could never be used in a tournament and do not afford full protection, they are not a good buy for an individual who cares enough about fencing to invest in his own clothing.

Jackets may be made of heavy gabardine, duck, or canvas. Most women prefer the gabardine which looks nice and tends to be more comfortable to wear. Some women's jackets have the necessary padding sewn in as part of the garment, and some have an extra vest of heavy quilted material which is worn under the outer jacket. In any case, women are required to have breast protectors of rigid material in addition to their jacket padding. Men may choose any of the fabrics, but if they plan to use épée, the duck or canvas will be necessary as the gabardine will tear more easily because of the stiffer blade of the épée.

The jacket should fit as snugly as possible without restricting movement. If a jacket is too large there will be loose cloth which will make it easier for a point to catch on the fabric. Left-handed fencers should buy jackets which button on the right side and are heavily padded on the left.

TROUSERS

According to the rules, fencing trousers must be white and must fasten below the knees. While it is best to wear regulation trousers which are lightly padded on top of the leading thigh, you may begin fencing with any white trousers which will allow freedom of movement and will protect the legs. Later you can purchase fencing knickers which match the jacket, allow for a maximum of motion, resist tearing, and look nice.

GLOVE

The foil glove should be of soft leather with a cuff which completely covers the lower part of the jacket sleeve. The glove may be lightly padded on the back. There may also be two thicknesses of leather on the end of the thumb and at the base of the thumb where the most wear occurs.

FOIL

When selecting a foil you should pick one which is neither too heavy and inflexible nor too light and whippy. The foible of the blade should readily bend or the blade may soon break, but if the blade is overly flexible the point will be difficult to control.

If you will be fencing with electric foils at all, you should practice either with an electric foil or with a dummy electric blade which is weighted the same as the electric foil, but is less expensive. The dummy blade can be put into any standard mounting. It is a mistake to buy a light standard foil for practice if you will fence with the electric blade because accuracy will be lost when you switch from a light to a heavy weapon, and you will tire more easily if you are not used to the extra weight. Every fencer should, if possible, have two foils so that if one breaks there is a spare.

MASK

A good quality mask is an absolute necessity for safety's sake. A new, medium weight mask will be adequate since the wire mesh must conform to strict standards. The mask should be white or of a light color as specified in the rule book. The price of masks varies somewhat but this is partly because of the various trims used. Canvas and plastic trim is the least expensive and will serve quite well. Leather trim is more costly, more

How can you prolong the life of your fencing clothing and equipment?

Evaluation Questions

durable and looks a little better, but it is not necessary. A plastic interior trim is the easiest to keep clean but it is not quite as comfortable to wear as cloth. In any case, the bib should contain several thicknesses of material to protect the neck. The mask should feel comfortable to the wearer and be secure.

If a man wishes to fence épée or sabre as well as foil, there are three-weapon masks which have a heavier mesh and afford more protection for the top and back of the head.

Whenever any rust appears on a mask it should be discarded for safety reasons. A mask which has been weakned by rust may be pierced by a heavy hit which could result in a severe injury to the fencer. For this reason it is unwise to buy a used mask. This is a personal item which you will want to keep for your own use.

ELECTRIC EQUIPMENT

If you decide to purchase the items necessary for electric foil fencing, you will need at least one, and preferably two, electric foils and at least two body cords. When you enter any electric tournament you are required to have two weapons and body cords in working condition. The wires used in the foil and cord are relatively fine and do occasionally break. Advice as to the maintenance and repair of electric equipment can be obtained from the Armorer, an expert on such matters, who is required to be present at every electrically scored meet.

A metallic vest is required for electric foil fencing. There must be no tears in this vest and it must fit so that it exactly corresponds to the valid target. The vest may be plastic lined to insulate a perspiring fencer from receiving a mild shock when a point is made against him.

CARE OF EQUIPMENT

Fencing clothing will last longer and look better if it is kept clean. Jackets and gloves should be stored so that they will dry after they have been used.

Masks should also be kept clean and dry. Many masks have removable bibs to make laundering easier. If the bib does not snap out, it can be scrubbed without harming the mask if it is well dried after scrubbing. Never immerse the entire mask in water.

Foils should also be stored in a dry place to prevent the formation of rust. They may be hung, point down, or stored so that they rest on the pommel, but they should never rest on the point.

Fencing bags are available for carrying equipment, but if wet clothing, mask, foil, etc. are all left rolled together after use the clothing will mildew and the metal objects will soon rust. Transport equipment in the bags, but then remove it for permanent storage unless it is dry. With reasonable care your fencing equipment should last for many years.

Suggested References

Barbasetti, Luigi. *The Art of The Foil, With a Short History of Fencing*, New York: E. P. Dutton, 1932.

Cass, Eleanor Baldwin. *The Book of Fencing*, New York: Lothrop, Lee and Shepard Company, Inc., 1930.

Castello, Hugo and James. *Fencing*, New York: Ronald Press Co., 1962.

Castello, Julio Martinez. *The Theory and Practice of Fencing*. New York: Charles Scribner's Sons, 1933.

Crosnier, Roger. *Fencing With The Foil*, New York: Ronald Press Co., 1951.

————. *Fencing With The Electric Foil*, New York: A. S. Barnes and Company, 1961.

Deladier, Clovis. *Modern Fencing*, Annapolis, Maryland: United States Naval Institute, 1948.

Fencing Rules and Manual, edited by Jose R. de Capriles, Amateur Fencers League of America, Mass.: Heffernan Press Inc., 1965.

Vince, Joseph. *Fencing*, New York: Ronald Press Company, 1962.

Index